HELLO WORLD(S)!

From Code to Culture:
A 10 Year Celebration of Java™ Technology

2005 marks the 10th birthday of Java™ technology. Starting out as just a programming language, Java technology has exploded into a ubiquitous technology platform that today touches the lives of people everywhere. This 10th birthday celebration book tells the story of how Java technology came to influence technologists, then businesses, then consumers, and now has become the predominate software on the planet.

# FOREWORD

In the early 1990s, a small group of us from Sun Microsystems were given the opportunity to spend all of our time thinking of what "the next big thing in technology" would be. What we created was a hardware-independent software platform unlike any other. We thought it was pretty cool, and so did our developer friends. But at that time, I don't think that any of us really had any idea of what we had done, not to mention how it would change the world. I certainly know I didn't.

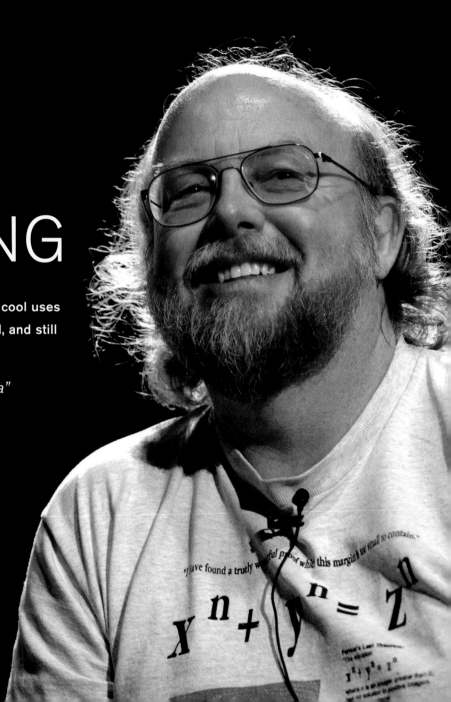

# BY JAMES GOSLING

And, of course, it wouldn't have happened if it weren't for the Java developer community. Developers are the ones who really made Java technology a success over the years. Their ingenuity, creativity, and millions of hours of contributed help has made the Java platform what it is today. We're lucky to have millions of developers constantly driving it forward into the future.

Every day I hear about new and cool uses for Java technology. I'm gratified, and still constantly amazed.

James Gosling *"Father of Java"*

# THE WORLD OF POSSIBILITIES

# 1991: WE'RE MISSING IT!

It was January 1991. The World Wide Web had yet to be born, a "browser" was someone who looks but doesn't buy, and the Internet was an arcane network used only by the military, government agencies, and uber-geeks. Standalone PCs ruled the earth and MS-DOS was the dominant operating system. Cell phones resembled a brick with an antenna – and could only make phone calls.

Sun Microsystems was the leading UNIX® OS workstation manufacturer, and was also doing well in network servers. Their tagline proclaimed The Network is the Computer™, but it was a concept that made sense to only a few back then. The idea that one day standalone computers would be obsolete and that all computers would be connected to a network was still new.

But big corporations, eager to grow their networks, understood, and Sun Microsystems could seemingly "stay its course" and thrive as the market grew.

"One day," says Gosling, "Patrick Naughton sent this ranting, primal-scream-of-frustration e-mail to Sun president Scott McNealy – '…Sun is really screwing up! We're missing a big change happening in technology!'"

Gosling recounts, "Well, Scott being Scott, he said,

"MAYBE YOU GUYS ARE ON TO SOMETHING….WHY DON'T YOU GO HIDE SOMEWHERE AND THINK ABOUT WHAT IT IS."

Quite a different opinion, however, was held by a gang of four "brilliant and bored" engineers at Sun Microsystems. They felt that Sun had lost some of its edge. The company wasn't living up to its technical potential, and as a result, neither were they. The group included Ed Frank, James Gosling, Patrick Naughton, and Mike Sheridan. They talked about leaving Sun for something more challenging, some place more in touch, some place that "got it."

So off they went, to anticipate and plan for the "next wave" in computing.

# BEHIND THE GREEN DOOR

Frank, Gosling, Naughton, and Sheridan set themselves up
in a secret off-campus office in Menlo Park above a Bank of America,
and away from Sun and corporate "antibodies."

Sun co-founder Bill Joy acted as the team's sponsor and oversaw the project from his Aspen, Colorado brain trust hideaway.

The office, which was entered through an unassuming green door, was basically one large room, which the team filled with lab benches, couches, and a refrigerator stocked with Dove Bars and Cokes. Amused that they actually worked "Behind the Green Door," they named themselves the Green Project. Newly energized, they analyzed where technology was headed and why it wasn't getting there faster.

They drank lots of coffee, and late into the night they toyed with, tested, and tore apart the computers, gadgets, and consumer devices of the day, looking for the direction of the next big thing.

But it was in a hot tub during a retreat near Lake Tahoe where the light bulb really came on. The four were soaking and drinking beer, talking about something they were noticing around them. Computer chips weren't just in computers anymore. Chips were starting to pop up in all sorts of consumer gadgets, from toasters to VCRs. Gosling commented that even the door knobs of their Squaw Valley ski lodge rooms had chips in them!

In that hot tub, it became apparent to the group that the true revolution would be linking all these devices together to create a world where consumer devices and computers were digitally connected. They stepped out convinced that that was the next wave – and they would tackle it.

# A TREE GROWS IN MENLO PARK:

As a first step in connecting consumer gadgets together, they wanted to create a device that could control a wide variety of everyday devices, in a sense a remote control on steroids. They began constructing a device they called "*7" (star seven).

They brought in several more developers, and each team member took a piece of the device puzzle – the hardware, the operating system, the networking, the interface, and the software application that would run on the device.

It was James Gosling who took on the task of writing the application for *7. What he quickly realized, however, was that existing programming languages wouldn't work for what he had in mind. If people were going to depend upon this language to run consumer products, it had to be more reliable and flexible than any other current languages.

The problem raised some essential questions about the nature of software. Why did applications have to be so big and cumbersome to write? Why couldn't an application run on different processor types without being rewritten? Why isn't there a sort of "application interpreter" that's the same for each operating system? That way, the same application code could run on different types of computers and devices.

# THE BIRTH OF **OAK.**

The problem sounded familiar – Gosling had seen something like this before. It took him back to software he had developed years ago in college. The same solution seemed to fit. Gosling immediately started writing a language and software interpreter that would model the idea. He based it on a set of essential software principles that he believed would be important to networked systems in general.

Weeks later, Gosling had written an "interpreter" in the form of a virtual machine made of software. He had also created a compact, simple software language, and the necessary code compiler, to drive the virtual machine. He called the new programming language "Oak", named for the tree outside his window.

**Gosling's original words used to describe Oak:** A simple, object-oriented, distributed, interpreted, robust, secure, architecture-neutral, high-performance, multithreaded, dynamic language.

In 1992, the Green team had grown to 13 members — all dedicated to bringing their remote control demo to life.

The team used Oak code to power the prototype — a wireless handheld computer with a large screen and no buttons. You turned the device on by touching the screen and controlled it by dragging your finger across the screen surface. Team member Mike Sheridan created a rule that the graphical user interface had to explain itself to the user, so anybody could use it immediately. The device's on-screen opening starred a molar tooth-shaped animated figure named Duke who explained everything you needed to know.

# A REMOTE CONTROL...

By August 1992, the Green team was ready to show their demo to Sun's president and CEO, Scott McNealy. What he saw was a device simple enough for anyone in the house to use, yet it would allow them to browse a TV guide, select a movie, finger-drag the movie to a VCR icon on the screen, and even program the VCR to record the show. In a world where most VCRs blinked "12:00," this caught his attention.

McNealy was blown away. Better yet, he allowed the group to set itself up as a wholly owned subsidiary of Sun Microsystems. The research project had become an engineering project, and First Person, Inc. was born.

# ...ON STEROIDS

*7 (star seven) was the name of the original demo that the group showed to Scott McNealy. The name was taken from the feature on the office phone system that lets users answer their phones from other extensions.

## A "WORKING" MASCOT

When the Green team emerged with a working demo of their interactive, handheld home entertainment controller, the heart of the animated touch-screen user interface was a cartoon character named Duke. The jumping, cartwheeling character was created by one of the team's graphic artists, Joe Palrang.

Duke was actually a representation of the "software agent" that performed tasks for the user. As such, Duke was the interactive host that enabled a new type of user interface that went beyond the buttons, mice, and pop-up menus of the desktop computing world.

Sure enough, Duke had staying power, and eventually he became the official mascot for Java technology. A living life-size "Duke" is also a feature at every JavaOne℠ Conference.

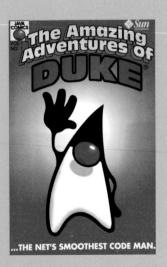

# SET-TOP BOXES...

The First Person team moved into a beautiful brick building in downtown Palo Alto at 100 Hamilton Avenue. Everything they needed – a commuter train and 24-hour food and coffee – was within a block.

The team was anxious to apply Oak and the principles established in their demo device to a revenue-generating market solution. In the first half of the 90s, the concept of an "information superhighway" had started to take hold, and many believed that interactive TV would be its on-ramp. The team decided they needed a foothold in the emerging digital cable industry. Set-top boxes and the concept of "video on demand" would be a natural fit for their technology, which was built around the concepts of networks.

The team began working on a new demo: MovieWood. While their previous demo content had been displayed on a sophisticated remote control screen, MovieWood provided a set-top box whose content was displayed on the TV screen. MovieWood would serve to link television to the information superhighway.

Using just a standard remote control, you could view a list of programs, change channels, and order and record shows over the network.

This functionality anticipated what TiVo would deliver publicly years later.

As luck would have it, Time Warner, via a project called the Orlando Trials, was planning a big push into interactive television and had issued a Request for Proposal on just such a technology. The cable company wanted to issue a set-top box to every one of their subscribers. They were interested in MovieWood, enthusiastic, and gave assurances. Months later, however, they pulled out at the last minute.

*100 Hamilton Avenue in downtown Palo Alto where First Person's offices were located.*

# ...THAT'S THE TICKET?

The setback almost sank Oak and First Person, which had grown to 50 engineers and specialists. A series of sales presentations to other companies in the cable TV and telecommunications industries also failed.

After two years of refinement and pitches, the team still couldn't find a market for their invention. No one was ready to go digital. Many cable companies feared they'd lose control of the viewer. The technology was revolutionary, viable, but maybe just a little bit ahead its time. No thank you.

By the middle of 1994, First Person was collapsing. Sun was ready to cancel the project and reassign the team. About a third of First Person began work elsewhere in Sun. Many simply left for other companies.

But about a dozen members quietly stayed in the building, hoping no one would notice, and continued developing the Oak language and platform.

They were depressed and exasperated, but still emotionally committed to Oak. It was just too cool to forget.

# THE WORLD OF CHOICE

# C++ +?

When team supervisor Bill Joy first saw Oak back in 1992, he knew it was the computer language he had been looking for as a replacement for the standard language "C" and its heir apparent C++.

Gosling says, "C++ was so widely accepted as the language we all had to use that most people didn't question it. But almost nobody liked it." Oak looked like it had the potential to replace C++ in many types of applications.

Joy says, "When James Gosling first showed me Oak, it was raw, but it had all the potential to really mean something." And if anyone would know that, it would be Bill Joy. In his graduate years at UC Berkeley, Joy had rewritten the standard AT&T UNIX operating system into a version he named Berkeley UNIX. Because his version was more stable and performed far better than the original, Berkeley UNIX soon became the new standard. Then he co-founded Sun Microsystems and led teams that transformed his Berkeley UNIX into Sun's operating system.

Like Gosling, Joy had wanted to find a language that was simple, comprehensible, and would run consistently across all operating systems –

"IN THE SAME WAY THAT AN EQUATION YIELDS THE SAME RESULT FOR ALL MATHEMATICIANS. A LANGUAGE LIKE THAT WOULD MEAN SOMETHING," HE SAYS.

Both of the early demos showed Oak had that potential.

# SANITY CHECK IT AT WICKED.NEATO.ORG

Before they turned anything loose to the world at large, however, there was a lot of work to be done. By the end of 1994, the team wanted to give their fellow developers on the outside world a glimpse at what they had been working on. They were looking for objective feedback, and needed to make sure that they weren't merely talking to themselves.

At this point, they had stable versions of the Oak compiler (the software that translates the program language into machine language that the computer can read) and their own Web browser that they had created using Oak.

What was unique about the Oak browser was that it contained software (the Oak "run-time environment") that allowed small applications to run securely within a Web browser. They named these small browser-based applications "applets."

In a near-unanimous decision, the team decided to release the technology to a few select friends over the Internet.

They loaded the Oak compiler and browser onto a Web site – wicked.neato.org – that Bill Joy maintained in Aspen and called a few developer friends to download it. Enthusiastic e-mails flew back in almost immediately. A soft buzz had begun.

From that point on, the team was newly energized.

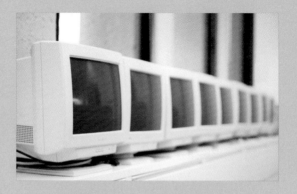

## THE SANDBOX: SECURITY BUILT INTO THE ROOTS OF OAK

From the beginning, Oak was designed as a software platform that would work across networks. However, unlike software that was designed to "stay put" on one computer, with this model came the threat of attacks and viruses. This meant that security had to be built into the platform from the start, otherwise the technology, as interesting as it was, would never survive.

The solution that was chosen was the "sandbox" model, which basically allowed users to download untrusted code over the network and run it in a secure environment. This model, along with the verifier, which catches most viruses or worms from the start, prevents viruses from infecting the system or the reading and writing of files from the hard drive. This ability is what made the Oak platform, and eventually the Java platform, so unique. As the platform evolved, various security levels were introduced so that any type of Java code (rather than just applets) could be run without fear of doing harm to the host system.

A couple of months later, in early 1995, John Gage, director of Sun's Science Office, stuck his head into James Gosling's office and said, "James, I need a SCSI cable, do you have one?"

# NO LONGER IS THE INTERNET FLAT

Gosling grabbed some from the team's stockpile. "Now, I need a couple of desktop systems. Can I borrow these?" No problem. Gosling offered to help carry them down to the car, asking along the way, "John, what are you doing with these systems?"

Gage answered that he had been invited to give a talk at the TED (Technology, Entertainment, and Design) Conference over the hill in Monterey, California. The distinguished TED audience was an eclectic and highly selective mix of technology gurus, scientists, artists, musicians, and TV and movie moguls. Gage had downloaded the team's custom-built browser and was going to demon-

strate it to this exclusive audience. Gosling, horrified at the prospect of the still rough browser crashing in a major public demonstration, jumped into Gage's full-of-gear Volvo and rode along to be his "demo dolly."

During Gage's presentation, Gosling operated a Sun workstation displaying the browser on a big screen. But he noticed that many people were only casually paying attention. Gage, a polished and engaging speaker, was telling the audience that this new technology would "bring the static Web to life," but it wasn't registering. They just weren't reacting.

Then, Gosling moused the cursor over a color illustration of a 3D molecule in the browser, clicked on it, and rotated the molecule back and forth. The entire audience went Aaaaaaah! "Their view of reality had completely changed because it MOVED," he says.

Far from the crash-and-burn scenario Gosling had first envisioned, the demo had jolted a very influential audience off their seats, and they were now delivering enthusiastic applause. Suddenly, everyone in the room was rethinking the potential of the Internet.

Software people stepped forward asking, "Could we build more sophisticated programs with this?" TV execs were asking, "Could we have dynamic interaction with our audience?" TV producers were asking incredulously, "…so this means our viewers could 'broadcast back' to us? We could have the news interact with viewers?"

"Yes, yes, and yes," was Gage's answer.

## BROWSERS: WEBRUNNER AND HOTJAVA™

In order to demonstrate Oak technology, as well as create a vehicle that would get their software into as many hands as possible, the Green team developed their own Web browser, WebRunner, named as an homage to the movie BladeRunner. It was created with Oak code and ran Oak applications. Later, when Oak became Java technology, the browser was renamed the HotJava™ browser. The group had originally wanted keep the WebRunner name, but when they received a letter from a lawyer at Taligent saying that they had already trademarked it, they moved to align the name with the Java brand.

# THE WORLD OF CURIOSITY

In preparation for going public, the team wanted to legally register the name Oak. What they found out, however, was that the name had already been taken by Oak Technologies.

# WHAT'S IN A NAME

In a panic, they arranged for a moderated brainstorming session to come up with an alternative. James Gosling characterizes that meeting as "continuous wild craziness." He explains, "Lots of people yelled out words. It felt like most of the words in the dictionary were yelled out at some time or another. There was a lot of 'I like this because...' and 'I don't like this because...'"

In the end, the long list was whittled down and a short list of the most popular candidates was turned in to the legal department. The instructions that accompanied the list were to go with which ever name looked legally "cleanest." The last thing the group wanted to do was to go with a name that they might have to change again. As Gosling tells it, "we told legal, strike out the ones that don't work. As soon as you get to one that works, we're taking it, no more debates, we're done."

That name was "Java."

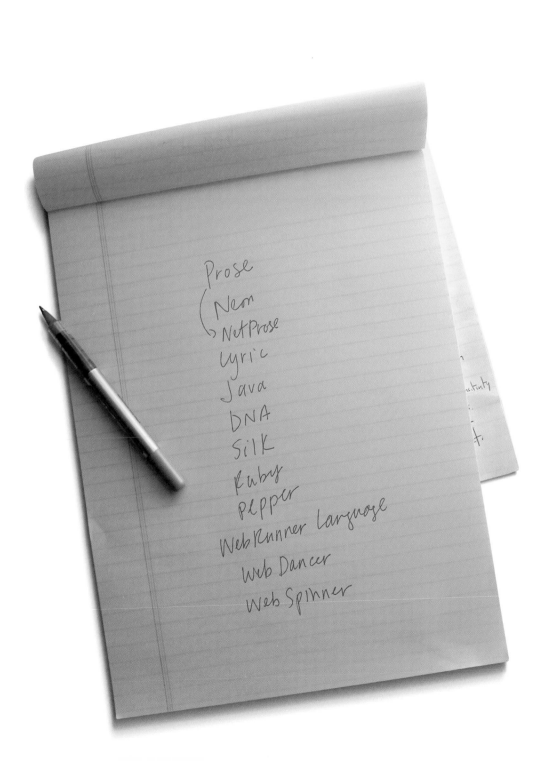

Prose
Neon
NetProse
Lyric
Java
DNA
Silk
Ruby
Pepper
WebRunner Language
Web Dancer
Web Spinner

## WHAT IF IT WASN'T "JAVA"?

Some of the other names on the original brainstorming list were:

Silk, DNA, Lyric, Pepper, NetProse, Neon, Ruby, WebRunner Language, WebDancer, WebSpinner

# WRITE IT ONCE AND RUN IT ANYWHERE

The more the team engineers worked with Java code, the more they saw its flexibility. They soon realized that this new platform could expand the limited options and choices everyone has in applications, operating systems, the Internet, and even hardware. It would be a clear challenge to Microsoft's Windows OS, which could only run applications that had been specifically written or adapted for it.

If you could write an application once and it would run on a lot of different types of computers, devices, and operating systems, that would exponentially increase the audience you could reach. Write Once, Run Anywhere™. In essence, any browser, any operating system, or any processor that could run the Java platform would be able to run Java applications. This capability, plus the reach that the rapidly growing World Wide Web provided, created a potential opportunity for mass adoption on a scale never seen before.

Suddenly, the full potential of Java technology grew too big to comprehend. Making objects in a browser jump and move was nothing compared to its potential to power up practically any type of digital device and let you control it over a network.

The idea was as big as technology itself. Everywhere the team looked, they could visualize new applications, new markets, and new industries.

There was no turning back at this point.

## HOW DOES IT RUN EVERYWHERE?

In order for an application to run on a computer, a different version of it must be rewritten (or "ported") for each specific operating system and chip combination. For example, an application written for use on a machine running Microsoft Windows with an Intel chip has to be rewritten to work on a computer that uses Mac OS and a PowerPC chip. What Java technology provides is a "virtual machine" that acts as a translator between the application and the OS/chip combination. This means that as long as a Java Virtual Machine has been created for a specific operating system/chip combination – and this only has to be done once – any program that works with the Java Virtual Machine will work there.

# BLACK AND WHITE AND READ ALL OVER

Then "it" happened. Team member Lisa Friendly tells the story: "It was Wednesday, March 22, 1995, and Lisa Poulson, who handled our PR, had arranged for the San Jose Mercury News to write a story on Java technology based on our upcoming official announcement. We all wore lots of hats back then. In addition to working on some developer and end-user docs, I was responsible for designing the new Web site, java.sun.com. Kim Polese, the Java product manager, had come by my office to tell me that we needed to have something linked with www.sun.com by Sunday when the article would run."

Friendly continues: "I thought, no problem. This gives me four days to get it ready – weekends were just additional workdays back then. In Internet time, that was a lifetime. I had leisurely started to put it together on Wednesday while working on my other projects. Then on Thursday morning at 7:30, I went to the driveway to pick up the paper and saw the front page of the Mercury. There it was. Uh-oh. Better get to the office in a hurry."

The front-page story positioned Java technology as "The Next Big Thing." It even included a quote from the Internet's wunderkind, Netscape's Marc Andreessen, giving the nod to Java technology as "great stuff."

Not only was the story supposed to run on Sunday, but it was expected to run in the business section, not the top half of the Mercury News front page. Friendly recalls: "I rushed into the office and worked as fast as I could. But people kept calling and knocking on my door to ask if I knew the story had run with a URL for which there were no Web pages! You know the term 'positive stress?' I was focused and ener-gized, but at the same time I thought I was going to become physically sick at my keyboard." She got the Web site up and running in a couple of hours.

From that day onward, that was the new pace for the entire Java software team.

Tim Lindholm, a team engineer, says, "It was just crazy. I was receiving 2000 e-mails a day and sending code updates out to 25,000 developers – all curious about a technology that hadn't even been announced by Sun Microsystems."

33

# THE FIRST RELEASE – LET'S GET SOME APPLICATIONS DEVELOPED

With the cat out of the bag, the team decided to take a big gamble. Days after the Mercury News story broke, the team released a full-public alpha, or early stage, version of the Java binary code over the Internet – for free.

The idea was to get people developing applications for the platform. They hoped that releasing free code to developers would help create widespread adoption. And it did. "Within an hour, I had developed a basic application with the Java language, and it was amazing," says programmer Amy Fowler, who later joined the Java team. Her husband, John Fowler also joined. Slowly but surely more applications began to come in. These initial applications were just the first of thousands and thousands that would be developed over the years to come by developers around the world.

In the beginning though, this growing popularity became a problem. James Gosling remembers, "I had to pick a number for Sun managers that represented success for Java technology. I said,

**" OK, IF WE REACHED 10,000 DOWNLOADS OF THIS FIRST RELEASE — 10,000 PEOPLE KICKING THE TIRES — WE WOULD BE A TOTAL, BLOW-THE-DOORS-OFF SUCCESS. "**

In just a couple of months, they flew past their goal.

The spiraling volume of e-mail inquiries and continuous downloads was beginning to tax the team's Internet connection. They constantly needed more bandwidth to satisfy the market's interest. It wasn't long, in fact, before they were getting more traffic than the rest of Sun combined.

Very quickly, the team's pace of life changed. Public attention brought action items and mountains of technical work to complete. The basic application programming interfaces were still under development. There was very little documentation. There was no support line for developer questions. Staff meetings and inter-views chewed up precious development time. But the code was out, and daily, the downloads continued to surge — all with virtually no marketing budget or plan.

# THE WORLD OF COMMUNITY

# DISASTROUSLY SUCCESSFUL

The first half of 1995 was a wild ride. The idea of bringing animation, interaction, and network applications to the static World Wide Web was a very powerful one. And now it was gaining enough developer support to take the Web to the next level – of motion, engagement, and two-way communication.

James Gosling is the first to admit it: "There was so much work to do that we knew we couldn't do it ourselves." In fact, they couldn't have hired enough programmers to do it.

It takes hundreds of thousands of hours to document, debug, test, port, and professionalize a software platform for global use in multiple languages. That's if everything goes smoothly – and it never does.

Carla Schroer, the team's first quality control manager, recalls it in dualities. "We were a full-blown success disaster. We were beyond-our-wildest-imaginations successful. And we were completely unprepared and understaffed to deal with all the attention we got and all of the work we needed to do. A lot of it was really fun and a lot of it was really painful. I wouldn't give up having done it for anything in the world, and I never want to do it again."

But there was no way they were going to give up.

# WITH A LITTLE HELP FROM OUR FRIENDS

In a bold move for the time, the team decided to offer the Java source code to developers over the Internet – for free. As James Gosling explains,

" ONE OF THE PHRASES WE USED A LOT WAS 'TOM SAWYERING.' WE DIDN'T HAVE ANYWHERE NEAR THE AMOUNT OF RESOURCES IT WOULD TAKE TO BUILD WHAT THE WORLD SEEMED TO WANT. SO WE JUST ENLISTED THE WORLD. "

Specifically, the tiny team needed help with ports (the adapting of the platform for specific systems), particularly to systems that they did not have access to and wouldn't have time to port to, and bug fixes, of which there were plenty to be made. The team was also looking for an objective evaluation of the technology's approach to security, which was different from what anybody had seen at the time. As Tim Lindholm, who led the source release program, describes it, "it foreshadowed some of the open-source philosophy of today, and was motivated by many of the same needs." In April of 1995, the code was released and the Java community began to grow.

Unbeknownst to the team, he and a couple of other Sun senior executives had been negotiating with Netscape's Marc Andreessen throughout the night.

# THE OFFICIAL BIRTH OF JAVA TECHNOLOGY...

Scott McNealy and other managers in Sun Microsystems had seen enough to commit. They decided to announce Java technology to their customers during the keynote speech at the upcoming SunWorld™ Conference.

It was May 23, 1995, and McNealy described the new technology to the conference crowd. Their enthusiastic response was more than he expected, and he still had a surprise up his sleeve.

McNealy signaled for Andreessen to come onstage. Andreessen and Netscape were well-known and highly regarded throughout the industry, especially to Sun customers. After all, they turned the Internet from an esoteric place used by academics and scientists to a tool accessible to the general public, first with their Mosaic browser, then again with the vastly improved Netscape Navigator™ browser. Sitting behind the easily accessible power of the Netscape browser, the Web had become a phenomenon that was impossible to ignore.

Andreessen took the microphone and announced that the next release of the browser, Netscape Navigator 2.0, would come with embedded Java technology. This was just the endorsement the fledgling technology needed. The crowd went wild. The final handshake on the agreement had come in the wee hours of that morning.

# DON'T SLEEP YET

The team went back to the office and threw themselves into readying the platform for the release of Netscape Navigator 2.0. They had only a few months to prepare for the submission deadline.

They began by adding fundamental enhancements that would ensure that the Java language was extensible and broadly applicable while retaining its essential simplicity, compact size, and predictability. Most importantly, compatibility was critical to maintaining the integrity of the Java platform. It had to run the same way on every platform that supported Netscape Navigator.

Carla Schroer says, "There were code bugs everywhere and we knew it, but we had to make the decision to focus on finishing the application programming interfaces, the essential methods programmers use to develop applications using the Java language. We knew we would all have to live with the fundamental decisions we made here. We could catch bugs later."

> " THE PROBLEM WAS, WE KNEW WE COULDN'T AFFORD TO MISS THE NETSCAPE NAVIGATOR DEADLINE. WAITING FOR THE NEXT RELEASE WASN'T AN OPTION. WE'D MISS THE MARKET. "

If the team hadn't been working hard enough before, they certainly were now. But, by the skin of their teeth and with a little help from the ability to "adjust" the time stamp of their submission, they made the deadline. Netscape Navigator 2.0 shipped with Sun's Java technology.

## WHAT, NO JAVA BOOKS?

James Gosling was traveling to meet a potential Java technology partner overseas. He stepped into a large bookstore to pick up some reading material. He went to the computer section, but he couldn't find a single book on Java technology. So he asked for help. The clerk led him back to the computer section and around the other side of the aisle. Indicating a wall-sized section of its own, he said, "This is our selection of Java books, sir."

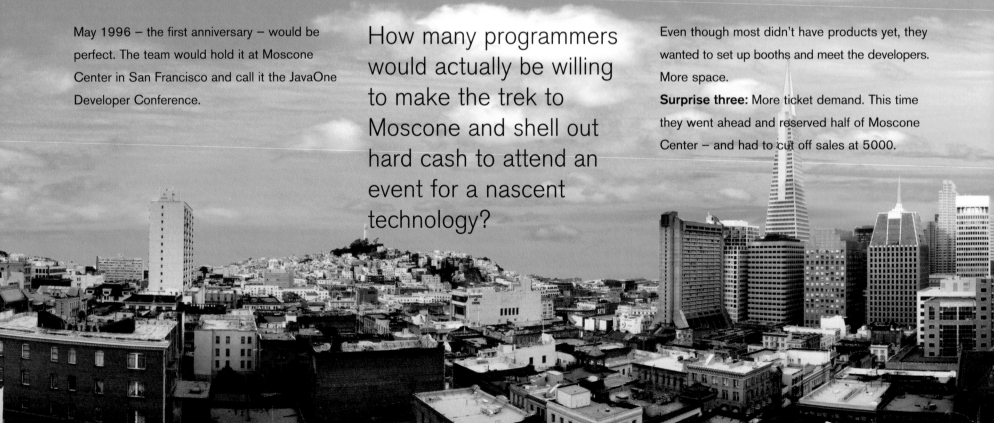

As 1996 arrived, the momentum of the Internet was sweeping up everything in its path – the press, governments, universities, businesses, and finally, consumers. Among the leaders of this movement was a new Java ecosystem of educators, authors, developers, tool providers, and licensees. They brought the Internet alive with interactive, browser-based "applets" written in the Java language that helped attract millions of Internet users. It was time for a Java conference.

The team had grown to just 50 people, stretched to the limit. A new team manager, George Paolini, took a look at the plan for the conference, months away, and threw a red alert. "We were really in trouble," says Paolini. He got involved immediately, as did everyone on the team eventually. Part of the problem is that they couldn't predict the attendance by the size of the Java online community.

Netscape had recently held their first developer conference and had approximately 1500 attendees. The Java technology team felt that if they could match this number they would have a huge success on their hands.

**Surprise one:** The reservations flooded in. They sold out almost immediately and had to reserve more conference space to offer more tickets.

**Surprise two:** The independent Java technology partners asked to have a show pavilion.

# IF WE HAD A CONFERENCE....

May 1996 – the first anniversary – would be perfect. The team would hold it at Moscone Center in San Francisco and call it the JavaOne Developer Conference.

How many programmers would actually be willing to make the trek to Moscone and shell out hard cash to attend an event for a nascent technology?

Even though most didn't have products yet, they wanted to set up booths and meet the developers. More space.

**Surprise three:** More ticket demand. This time they went ahead and reserved half of Moscone Center – and had to cut off sales at 5000.

At the conference, the Java Development Kit (JDK™) 1.0 was unveiled as the toolkit for building applications using the Java language, and ten operating system providers announced the intent to license Java technology.

"We expected to be clobbered by the attendees for all the bugs and the unfinished parts of the platform," says Carla Schroer. "But instead, it was a 'love-fest.' They thought what we were doing was great."

**Overwhelmed With Attention**

Word spread, and the community grew quickly from the first JavaOne Conference onward. Two months later, in July 1996, 50,000 people attended "Sun Java Day" in Tokyo. By the end of the year, it was estimated that 83,000 Internet pages were using Java technology. Downloads of Java technology had reached 220,000 developers. And everyone wanted more information.

The second JavaOne Conference, held in April 1997, attracted 8000 attendees and became the largest gathering of software developers ever. In 1998, it grew to 15,000, and by 1999, it had hit the maximum capacity of Moscone Center at 20,000.

# ...WOULD ANYONE COME?

# THE WORLD OF ADOPTION

# STEP RIGHT UP AND GET YOUR LICENSE

As the year 1996 began, Sun created an official JavaSoft business unit and hired Alan Baratz as its president. Baratz was an MIT doctoral graduate and IBM researcher. Java technology had captured his interest, but running the new JavaSoft division of Sun required all of his concentration.

Baratz describes the momentum when he joined in January: "1995 ended with the announcement of the Letter of Intent between Sun and Microsoft to license Java technology for inclusion in Internet Explorer. So now you had the two main browsers – Internet Explorer and Netscape Navigator – agreeing to incorporate Java technology." This fact, coupled with the success of the first JavaOne Developer Conference, created...

...a landslide of companies wanting to license Java technology – including everyone from one-man shops to industry giants like Apple, HP, and IBM. Baratz and his team quickly found themselves signing up licensees as fast as they could.

*BOSTON, MA – AUGUST 5, 1997: Apple Computer CEO Steve Jobs at computer, working on his Macworld Expo speech while on a cellular phone. Apple was one of the industry giants to sign up for a Java license.*

# IF IT ISN'T COMPATIBLE...

While the ubiquity of the Java platform was the main goal, it was also critical during this period of mass licensing that it be built on the same "flavor" of Java technology.

A stampede of licensees helped drive greater-adoption of the Java platform among developers and their customers, which was crucial for its survival. Developers aren't interested in spending their time writing applications based on a language available to only a few. And if the developers didn't create applications, end users wouldn't be interested in the platform either.

Large companies – such as Microsoft, IBM, HP, Oracle, and Novell – wanted a lot of flexibility to adapt the Java platform, but at the same time it was imperative that they adhere to strict compatibility standards. If one of the licensees decided to create a version of the platform for their particular operating system and broke compatibility, that implementation would divide the market and destroy the platform's "Write Once, Run Anywhere" promise. Java technology had to be the same everywhere.

In order to identify proper implementations of the Java platform, the "Java Compatible™" logo was created. Licensees could display this on their products only if the product was certified to adhere to the Java platform specifications and APIs without proprietary, vendor-specific changes.

JAVA™
COMPATIBLE

*The original Java Compatible logo used to identify proper implementations of the Java platform.*

## IBM: An Endorsement With Authority

Simon Phipps, now Sun's chief technology evangelist, was a technical program manager at IBM when Java technology was introduced. He was given the assignment of evaluating this new platform to see if it was a viable solution for IBM's situation: The IBM software labs were being stretched thin supporting a variety of operating systems – OS/2, AIX, OS/400, and System 390. "Those were just the active operating systems," quips Phipps. "They had 15 more they were in various stages of decommissioning."

Conceptual similarities between IBM's VM (Virtual Memory) operating system and Java technology gave them a head start in under-standing and embracing the ideas behind Java technology. "That made it extremely easy to persuade people in IBM that if Java technology actually worked, it would be a good way of hiding the platform differences and making a much smaller, more effective range of software."

Because the Java technology source code was available from Sun, Phipps' team at Hursley Park, England was able to download it and port it to OS/2 and AIX during the summer of 1995. "By Autumn, we were convinced that it was going to be a great technology," says Phipps. "We wrote a report explaining what Java technology was, how it worked, and what the opportunity was for IBM. We easily gained approval to proceed with the porting activity."

The key to Phipps' quick success was the fact that the Sun Java team had made the Java source code freely available over the Internet. "That made it very easy for a little skunk works group like ours at IBM to download it and prove that it would be useful without asking for permis-sion or going through negotiations." They even ported Java technology to Windows 3.1.

Near the end of the 1990s, Java technology had fully achieved the objectives we wanted for it – to unify IBM's software division," says Phipps.

# ...IT ISN'T JAVA

# THE OPERATING SYSTEM FOR THE INTERNET

By 1997, the Internet was on everyone's mind as something that could change the world. And Java technology, with the interaction it brought to the static Web, made good news for Internet users and developers, large and small.

Influential technology columnist George Gilder had written an article about Java technology that put the stamp of approval on the growing momentum. It was published in Forbes ASAP, August, 1995. Team marketing manager George Paolini says, "It was this article that really took a step back, looked objectively at Java technology, and said, 'This is the first sort of universal operating system. This is the operating system for the Internet.'"

Paolini admits, "The first couple of versions of Java technology were pretty crude. There was a lot of functionality missing, and what worked had a lot of room for improvement. But developers could set that aside because they believed in the value of being able to write an application once and have it run on multiple devices. That promise alone was enough to carry them forward and believe in the technology, to invest their time and money."

Guy Steele, an early team member who worked with Bill Joy to write the language specification, says that the early success of Java technology was both push and pull. "Sun put a lot of effort behind Java technology development and marketing, but it wouldn't have gotten anywhere if it hadn't filled a huge need. The Java platform provided a way to program the Internet. It had a good security story, it was close enough to C++ that it was easy to switch, but it was easier to use than C++, and it provided great APIs for user interfaces, network connections, talking to browsers, and organizing business applications. It was what people needed to make e-commerce happen."

Now the buzz was spilling over beyond software developers and Internet providers. It hit Internet consumers like a fever.

The business and consumer press made it glow. The Internet and Java technology were the new way to the future. Java "hype" took on a life of its own. One team member overheard a man in his 70s saying, "I want to get a computer, but it's gotta have that Java in it. That's what I want. Java." When asked what Java is, he replied, "I'm not sure, but that's what I want!"

## JAVA: DON'T LEAVE COLLEGE WITHOUT IT

When Java technology was introduced, one of the first requirements was a developer community that had acquired the skills to code Java applications. From the beginning, a large number of universities wanted to include Java courses in their offerings, but their instructors weren't themselves qualified in the brand new technology.

But before long, instructional development books hit the shelves, and Web sites dedicated to Java coding sprang up. By 1997, research firm Gartner Group found that Java programming was being taught in 78 percent of the surveyed universities and colleges in the U.S., and was mandatory in 50 percent of the Computer Science programs. One professor explains that after the first semester, they had produced enough advanced students to serve as teaching assistants, enabling them to expand their curriculum.

Not only did students find a "fun factor" in Java programming, but both they and the teachers realized that Java programming would be a valuable skill to posses when entering the job market.

Today, almost every college and high school that provides programming courses offers Java programming, and it is even being seen in junior high schools worldwide.

## SPREADING THE GOOD WORD

Sun appointed one of the JavaSoft team members, Miko Matsumura, as a Java evangelist and set him loose. Matsumura, with straight black hair that hung below his shoulders, traveled the world, meeting with technology, business, and government leaders explaining the benefits of Java technology. Quickly, his audiences grew to thousands.

Matsumura says, "We never suspected the rocket ride Java technology would turn out to be. In a few short years, I had logged a half-million frequent flyer miles and was transported from Johannesburg to Jakarta in an all-out effort to evangelize this new technology."

TRAVEL LOG: MATSUMURA, MIKO

| Date | Location | Event |
|---|---|---|
| 4-15-95 | Menlo Park | Ultra Launch Java Day |
| 5-30-95 | San Francisco | SunSoft Sales Training |
| 8-8-95 | Tokyo | Internet CyberWorld |
| 9-12-95 | New York City | Java Day |
| 2-28-96 | Santa Clara | Cisco's Java Day |
| 3-15-96 | Hanover | Java Day CeBIT |
| 4-8-96 | New York City | IntraNet 96 |
| 4-17-96 | San Jose | SUNsoft Technology Exchange |
| 4-24-96 | Tokyo | NTT UNIX Forum |
| 4-27-96 | Bangalore | Internet India '96 |
| 5-1-96 | Toronto | Java Day |
| 5-13-96 | New York | International Java Developers Conference |
| 5-15-96 | Boston | SunSoft Technology Exchange |
| 5-21-96 | Detroit | Novell Conference |
| 5-22-96 | Palm Springs | ESRI User's Conference |
| 5-29-96 | San Francisco | JavaOne Conference |
| 6-3-96 | Mexico City | Java Day |
| 6-26-96 | Seattle | Northwest Developer Conference |
| 7-9-96 | San Jose | Web Developer's Conference |
| 7-23-96 | Las Vegas | SUN NAFO Conference |
| 8-19-96 | Singapore | Enterprise Java Summit |
| 8-20-96 | Kuala Lumpur | Enterprise Java Summit |
| 8-26-96 | Bombay | Enterprise Java Summit |
| 8-29-96 | Jakarta | Enterprise Java Summit |
| 9-5-96 | San Jose | Reuter's 9th Unicode Conference |
| 9-6-96 | Monterey | Sun Service EduCamp |
| 9-13-96 | San Francisco | Seybold Java Rock Over Hype |
| 9-23-96 | Manila | InternetWorld |
| 9-23-96 | Manila | UNIX User's Group |
| 9-25-96 | London | Object Expo |
| 10-16-96 | San Francisco | Netscape Developers Conference |
| 10-31-96 | Ho Chi Mihn | Asia South Press Symposium |
| 11-6-96 | Jakarta | JavaStation Launch |
| 11-8-96 | Manila | JavaStation Launch |
| 11-20-96 | Las Vegas | COMDEX Panel |
| 12-4-96 | Tokyo | Java Day Winter 96 |
| 2-9-97 | Palm Springs | Demo97 |
| 2-11-97 | Bangkok | Net & Info |
| 2-26-97 | Seoul | Asia Internet Associates |
| 3-14-97 | Milan | Java Day Milan |
| 4-2-97 | San Francisco | JavaOne Conference |
| 4-8-97 | San Francisco | Web Market West |
| 4-10-97 | Singapore | NetWorld – Interop |
| 5-2-97 | Sacramento | Java User's Group |
| 5-9-97 | Berkeley | Java User's Group |
| 5-13-97 | San Francisco | Noend |
| 5-15-97 | San Francisco | CBT Panel |
| 6-2-97 | New York City | SIGS Java Expo NYC |
| 6-11-97 | London | EMPA London |
| 7-10-97 | San Diego | ESRI San Diego |
| 7-16-97 | Tokyo | Cosmos/Sunergy Tokyo |
| 7-23-97 | Chicago | InternetWorld |
| 8-13-97 | Kuala Lumpur | Java@work Malaysia |
| 8-18-97 | Bombay | Java@work Bombay |
| 8-20-97 | Bangkok | Thailand Assumption University |
| 8-26-97 | Johannesburg | Java South Africa |
| 8-29-97 | Cape Town | Java South Africa |
| 9-7-97 | Washington, DC | Software Publisher's Association |
| 9-9-97 | Chicago | SIGS JavaExpo |
| 9-30-97 | Kona | Hawaii 100% Pure Java |
| | | 100% Pure Java |
| | | Internet Associates Symposium |
| 11-21-97 | Copenhagen | Java Day Denmark |
| 12-12-97 | Philippines | Asia South Press |
| 3-22-98 | San Francisco | JavaOne Conference |
| 5-5-98 | Milan | 3rd Italian Java Conference |
| 5-11-98 | Nice | Novell Brainshare |
| 5-14-98 | Cannes | Film Festival |
| 5-26-98 | Tokyo | Java Developers Conference |
| 5-11-98 | Nice | Novell Brainshare |
| 5-14-98 | Cannes | Film Festival |
| 5-28-98 | Tokyo | Java Developer's Conference |

1 MAN

69 CITIES | 500,000 MILES

# EVERYTHING WITH A DIGITAL HEARTBEAT

Early in 1998, Scott McNealy was a keynote speaker at COMDEX, the king of Microsoft Windows PC shows. It seemed like an awkward fit. Generally, these Windows-bound business and consumer technologists didn't have much association with Sun, a big-business UNIX networking company. His first words were, "What am 'I' doing at COMDEX!" Waves of laughter swept over the crowd.

Java technology, of course, was the answer. McNealy entertained them with visions of a Java technology-powered world.

> **NOT JUST PCS, BUT EVERYTHING WITH A DIGITAL HEARTBEAT — FROM FLIGHT DATA RECORDERS, TO RACE CARS, TO YES, YOUR OWN PERSONAL CAR — WILL BE CONNECTED TO THE INTERNET.**

Java software, he explained, would play a key role. It was a strange and new thought to a telephone-line-tethered PC audience at the time.

But he had something that would help them understand and remember for good. He pulled out his Java technology-powered Palm Pilot and used it to remotely start the new red Cadillac on the other side of the conference hall. Being Scott, he also honked the horn and blinked the lights. Swells of applause filled the auditorium as a new user base enthusiastically "got it." Like the audience at the TED Conference, when John Gage and James Gosling first publicly demonstrated Java technology, this COMDEX crowd had some new thinking to do.

*SEOUL, SOUTH KOREA: A South Korean man looks at a technologically advanced car.*

# THE WORLD OF INEVITABILITY

Growth means change, and if the changes are the right ones, the organism survives. If not, the organism becomes extinct.

# THE RIGHT TIME FOR BIG BUSINESSES

The danger of Java technology evolving too quickly, or not quickly enough, was an ongoing issue. The essential core ideas made it popular, but would they carry the technology into the next century?

Even back in the fall of 1995, the team had set their sights on extending the Java platform outward to include connectivity with databases, servers, and other system resources.

Graham Hamilton, a Sun distinguished engineer, was the main proponent of the move to connect with the rest of the computing world, especially mainstream businesses. "Extending the Java platform represented a significant philosophical choice," he says. "We could have chosen to drive for a 'pure Java' solution where we tried to rewrite the whole world in Java code. But that didn't seem to reflect reality, especially in the enterprise. So we chose to deliberately focus on connecting into the existing world, with all its flaws, rather than going for an overly idealistic 'Java-only' approach. That's the foundation that eventually evolved into 'Enterprise Java.'"

### Java Technology Makes Great Glue

The team started with database connectivity and found a welcome reception by the major database vendors. These vendors wanted to make sure their products could connect to Java applications.

Then the team looked more broadly at ways in which Java technology could be used as "middle-ware" that could connect existing services. Hamilton says, "We found that the idea of Java technology as a unifying 'glue layer' that could connect a lot of different resources was a very powerful concept."

He adds, "The more you can connect and coordinate resources and access data from different sources, the more you can drive and support real business transactions. That was the idea behind what became Enterprise JavaBeans™ – a Java technology specification that enables easy-to-develop 'server-side' applications designed for secure, portable net-work-distributedtransactions. Only after that was launched did we start a complete Enterprise Java strategy." It was here, in the enterprise servers that power networks, that Java technology would make some of its greatest gains.

Interactive Web pages were one thing, but industrial-strength business networks could really benefit from the broad resource connectivity of Java technology.

# MORE HELP FROM OUR FRIENDS

The applications and platform improvements that resulted over the next few years were created through enormous coordination and work by a wide range of industry heavyweights, especially IBM, Microsoft, Oracle, and Sybase. Hamilton says,

**❝ THEY WANTED TO WORK WITH US TO CREATE A STANDARD THAT WOULD MAKE JAVA TECHNOLOGY SUCCESSFUL IN THE MARKETPLACE, AND THEIR INSIGHTS AND IDEAS WERE CRITICAL. ❞**

"It was that inclusive process, and its success, that eventually led to the creation of the Java Community Process℠ program."

**Adding Process to the Community**

In 1998, in order to evaluate and coordinate the various Java technology efforts that were underway around the world, Sun launched the Java Community Process (JCP™) program.

The JCP program gives participants the right to create new pieces of Java technology through community collaboration. By 1999, the JCP program, with its industrywide membership, had become the evolutionary force driving and controlling all changes to the Java platform as a community.

Today, as Java technology turns ten years old, there are over 900 members of the JCP program, and more than half of them are from outside the United States. Members include such industry leaders as Cisco, HP, IBM, Motorola, Nokia, Oracle, Siemens, and Vodafone. Participation, however, is not limited to large corporations, and in fact, one of its keys to success is the diversity of its membership, which also includes governments, universities, and individual developers as well as open source and non-profit groups.

As one of the most successful technology communities ever, the JCP program has become a recognized community model for sharing complex technical ideas and intellectual property globally.

# JAVA TECHNOLOGY NOW COMES IN THREE FLAVORS

In 1997, Java technology was growing so fast that the core team couldn't keep up with it.

James Gosling and Tim Lindholm would often discover books on Java topics they'd never heard of. "Java technology books" was one of the fastest-growing categories on Amazon.com, and the developer community had grown close to a million participants.

By 1998, the team and its industry partners were seeing vast horizons for Java technology, from very small applications running on handheld devices to very large applications running on networks that power banks and credit card companies.

"We were overwhelmed with the possibilities for Java technology," says Hamilton. "We increasingly came to realize that there needed to be focused areas of Java technology, each with full technical support for the marketplace."

They had also recognized the need to make some fundamental changes and radical improvements to the platform. More than a simple update was needed.

Through the Java Community Process program, the community decided to offer three distinct versions of the Java platform.

The needs of PC and Internet developers were different from the needs of enterprise developers. And, the fast-growing community of developers for "micro devices" – PDAs, mobile phones, and other consumer electronics – had their own special needs.

At the JavaOne Conference in June of 1999, Sun announced that the Java platform would now be available in three editions:

**The Standard Edition,** the core technology for desktop systems and servers

**The Enterprise Edition** for medium to large businesses

**The Micro Edition** for small and mobile devices such as cell phones and PDAs

Through the community's industrywide participation, which led to the three editions, the essential technology had become much more refined and sophisticated. The initial, rough Java language had become an integrated, feature-rich, ready-for-prime-time proposition. The real Java technology we know today had finally emerged.

The Micro Edition of Java technology made its public debut at the JavaOne Conference in June of 1999. NTT DoCoMo, one of the top wireless service providers in Japan, demonstrated prototype handsets running NTT's "i-mode" service that now delivered "phone-sized" Java applications.

# JAVA TECHNOLOGY GOES MOBILE

Since its inception, Java technology was intended to connect consumer devices to networks. While the technology had its first success on the desktop and then found its way to corporate servers, it took a little longer to gain traction in the micro-device space. But when it did, it made up for lost time.

Several months later, Java technology-powered cell phones arrived in Europe. Mobile Java technology continued to gather steam around the world when finally, in 2002, it reached the tipping point. On October 22nd of that year, the U.K.-based wireless provider, Vodafone, the industry's 800-pound guerilla, rolled out Java technology-powered applications to its 50 million consumers across Europe. With this rollout, Java technology had truly become a large scale consumer player. Today, the mobile device marketplace is one of the leading demand generators for Java technology.

**Over 2.5 billion Java technology-enabled devices.**
(Sun Microsystems, June 2005)

**Over 140 mobile operators worldwide have deployed Java services.** (Nokia, June 2005)

**Over 700 million Java technology-powered handsets sold by the end of June 2005.** (Ovum)

**Approximately 23 million mobile Java applications have been downloaded.** (Nokia, June 2005)

**Over 45,000+ mobile Java applications are currently on the market.** (Informa Telecoms & Media, June 2005)

## PUT IT ON MY CARD

The Micro Edition's "small footprint" application code prompted developers to ask, "How small can a Java application get?" Axalto, a provider of smart cards delivered the answer, at least for the time.

Axalto, which at the time was still part of the French conglomerate Schlumberger, designed and manufactured wallet-size cards with electronic capabilities for identity verification and financial transactions. Their engineers liked the potential of the Java platform, but even the Micro Edition code was too large for the memory constraints in their cards. So on their own, they engineered a stripped-down subset of the software that worked on a smart card. Then they made Sun an incredible offer.

Axalto would give their implementation of the "Java Card™" technology to Sun, who could then license it back to Axalto, who would pay a fee for the right to use it. Alan Baratz asked, "Why would they want to do that, give it to us for free, then pay us to use it?" The answer was that it had more market power for them as a Java implementation than a proprietary Axalto technology. The Java brand itself had become recognized and trusted in a way that meant value in the marketplace.

They showed James Gosling what Axalto had done, and he said that's the way he would have done it himself. That was good enough for Baratz. An agreement was reached with Axalto, and Java Card technology was launched, making Java technology available to dozens of smart card manufacturers who followed Axalto's lead.

# THE WORLD OF TODAY

Today, chances are that
Java technology touches
your life.

# JAVA EVERYWHERE

Java technology has become the essential ingredient of the digital experience for hundreds of millions of people in all walks of life, all over the planet. Java software powers the onboard computers in toys, cars, planes, and rockets. It even gave NASA's Mars Rover "eyes" by creating images out of data sent from onboard cameras. This provided scientists with a view of Mars and allowed them to select what to explore next.

Java technology brings interactivity to the Internet, real-time graphics to television, instant imaging to cameras, and multiplayer games to mobile phones. It connects the largest enterprises and smallest businesses to their employees, customers, and data. And it secures the vast majority of electronic transactions in retail, finance, government, science, and medicine. In short, Java technology goes everywhere you go.

*PASADENA, CA – JANUARY 25, 2004: Pete Theisinger, Project Manager, and Jennifer Trosper, Spirit Mission Manager for Surface Operations, react as the first images arrive from the NASA Mars Rover, "Opportunity," at Jet Propulsion Laboratory (JPL).*

# CONNECTING NATIONS

Java technology's ability to connect widely disparate systems makes it a prime candidate for projects on a national scale.

In South America, the Brazilian Healthcare System Project is tasked with providing universal healthcare to approximately 200 million people. The project will leverage Java technology to connect 236 previously disconnected systems, including a national patient database, hospitals, outpatient facilities, and pharmacies even in the remotest regions.

In Belgium, a project is being launched that will provide every resident of the country over 12 years of age with a personal ID card based on Java Card technology.

# JAVA TECHNOLOGY WORKING TODAY

MLB.com, which is one of the Internet's most heavily trafficked sites, offers more live events than any other Web site. In 2004, with the help of Java technology, MLB.com delivered more than 1 billion minutes of streaming media and 2430 full-length games to more than 1 billion visitors.

The world's premier online auction site, eBay, relies on Java technology to handle more than $1,000 per second in merchandise sales and more than 100 million registered users worldwide.

Japan's NTT DoCoMo takes consumer convenience to a new level with the i-mode FeliCa Mobile Wallet service. Enhanced by Java technology-based applications, it allows users to replace their cash, cards, and house key with a FeliCa contactless chip in their phones.

## THE JAVA BRAND: FROM GEEK TO CHIC

While originally known only by serious developers, the "Java" brand has grown to become one of the most well-known and respected brands in technology. It is recognized by 86 percent of tech-savvy consumers around the world, and, given the choice, one in three tech consumers prefers products that have Java technology to those that don't.

"The growth and market demand for the Java Powered brand has been overwhelming" said Ingrid Van Den Hoogen, Sun's vice president of Brand Experience and Community Marketing. "We see consumers using the brand to determine which games and software to play and buy, and device manufacturers from printers to cell phones all looking to display the Java Powered logo."

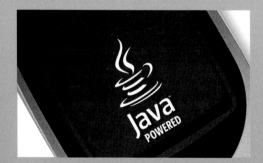

# SERIOUS BUSINESS: JAVA GAMES

There's nothing quite like a good game to get your fingers flying and heart racing.

And every new game "ups the ante" on entertainment value, so it keeps developers moving fast to compete with each other. Java technology is especially game-friendly for users, developers, and service providers.

No other software technology can deliver such fast and furious fun to mobile phones. That's why the June 2005 Wireless Gaming Review lists over 2700 Java games, and seven out of their top nine games were written in Java code. It's also why 140 mobile phone operators and carriers deploy Java technology to their customers.

Just take a look at the people around you at an airport, commuter train, muni bus, waiting room, or lunch room and you can watch the number of players multiply each month. Mobile gaming is big business, and is growing as fast or faster than any other Java technology marketplace.

What about at home? Desktop gaming is also a fast-growth specialty of Java technology. Browser-based online games are great entertainment for consumers and a lucrative worldwide market for developers and providers. Java technology allows users to play games online in real time as well as download games for offline play. That brings revenues to operators and licensing fees to developers.

*Just one of the thousands of Java technology-based games available on Java Powered mobile phones today.*

*Players use their cell phones to test each others' driving abilities on the world's first live-action, interactive video game on a billboard in Times Square in New York City.*

The global market for Java Powered products and services includes millions of consumers using digital devices and desktop systems as well as the majority of corporate enterprises using business-critical software.

# THE JAVA ECONOMY

Over 90 percent of the Fortune 500 depend on Java technology for some aspect of their business transactions. Approximately 4.5 million developers deliver these products and services using Java software – making Java technology the world's most popular software. The Java ecosystem has become an estimated $100 billion marketplace of its own.

After 10 years, has its popularity diminished? Absolutely not! Java technology is the software of choice for the majority of the planet's software engineers, and it is the most predominate software running today.

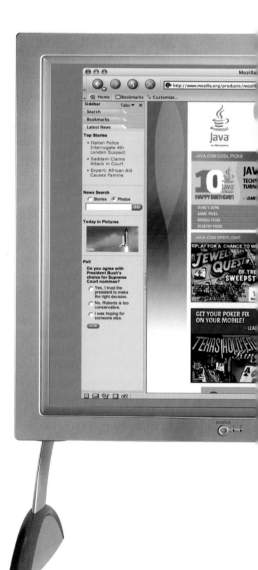

*java.com, visited by 12 million unique visitors a month, is Sun's consumer Web site that presents some of the coolest Java games and applications around.*

# THE WORLD OF TOMORROW

# JAVA SPEAKS NEW LANGUAGES

Which way will Java technology head in its second decade? What will it become? The evolution of Java technology is a collective effort, and no one knows for sure where it will go.

One direction various Java technology visionaries would like to see is for the platform to accommodate a wider range of developers by having new languages, in addition to the Java language, enabled to run on the Java platform.

Graham Hamilton predicts, "Looking out to 2010 and onto 2015, we expect the Java platform will have a very long life, and we expect entirely new, experimental languages will emerge that target many different types of developers in flexible ways."

"The Java language is almost unimportant compared to the Java Virtual Machine concept," says Gosling. "I can certainly imagine all kinds of languages running on the Java Virtual Machine."

Similarly, Bill Joy envisions worlds where 'fluid computing' might be based on Java Virtual Machines communicating. He explains that the current computing infrastructure of transactions based on file systems and databases could change to a system of "transactive datastructures" held in machine memory. Joy says that such a datastructure could possibly be 100 times faster than today's databases. "That would make a huge difference in our ability to be transactive, and in a sense, everything we do with machines is transactive."

Extremely high speed, low-overhead transactions would open the way for a whole new world of applications and enterprises unlike anything in existence today. "The closest thing we have today is online multiplayer games, which are probably more pioneering than anything corporations are doing these days."

Guy Steele agrees. "It's not enough to just accumulate a large amount of data and have access to it. You need to be able to correlate the data and find relationships within it. That becomes exponentially complex, but there is a big need for that type of structure. Both the language and the computational infrastructure will have to address that to make it happen."

# GREATER SOCIAL IMPACT

James Gosling sees Java technology as being a perfect fit to address many of the complexities of the future. "One of the long-term benefits of Java technology is being able to tie together a lot of resources on the network, from the network edge to the core. It is creating a unifying whole that is really exciting."

This fits with what some community members are envisioning as the Java "grid", which would serve as an interconnected tapestry of computing power that anyone could use. Such a grid could allow real-time communications, for example, to shorten disaster recovery response times by coordinating logistics and patient care.

Disease outbreaks could be greatly lessened or contained with integrated medical statistics to enable rapid trend recognition. Even matching organ donors and recipients could be done more quickly and with a higher success rate with the Java grid, saving more lives.

"THE THING I FIND MOST EXCITING OVER THE NEXT TEN YEARS IS THE WAY TECHNOLOGIES ARE BECOMING MUCH MORE PERVASIVE AND WOVEN INTO THE FABRIC OF EVERYDAY LIFE," SAYS GOSLING.

## THROUGH THE LOOKING GLASS

What if windows were translucent so you could see multiple windows at the same time? What if you could tack a note to yourself right on the Web page you're viewing? What if your CD or movie database became a 3D jukebox? Project Looking Glass is using Java technology-based developments to bring 3D windowing capabilities to the desktop, offering a far richer user experience for work and "play."

# HAVE YOUR MACHINE CALL MY MACHINE

Paul Saffo, Director of the Institute for the Future and long-time Java technology fan, has a similar vision.

He predicts that the percentage of human-to-human and human-to-machine transactions will be overshadowed by machine-to-machine transactions.

He explains that at first, all electronic conversations on the planet were between people. Then, suddenly in the 1990s, the number of network communications between a person and a machine grew much larger. Today, the number of electronic communications between humans is miniscule compared to those of humans communicating with the machines themselves. "Today, when we think of 'commerce,' we think of people buying things. But in the future, 'commerce' will also include machines doing transactions with each other, which may be the majority of all transactions." The "fluidity" of Java technology will be a primary enabler of this trend.

Saffo also warns that "the future" always comes later than is predicted and occurs in unexpected ways. When hypertext looked like the next big thing, cyberspace was what was actually coming our way. He believes that in the future, cyberspace will move out from its current "desktop and device" representation to embrace more of the real world. As an example, he says that whereas Google has indexed the Internet, at some point, much of the "real world" may be indexed, allowing us to find and deal with objects in reality. "And, of course, it will all be written in the Java language."

Over its ten-year existence, Java technology has increased the liquidity of computing. The easily distributed computation power of Java code has allowed computational processes to occur in new places and on new devices.

Saffo predicts that one of the most incredible opportunities for developers will be in robotics. He says, "There is a huge, pent-up demand among consumers for robots, especially cute, lovable intelligent robots that do something useful." Look for fluid connections between people, information, and devices, and you'll find Java technology at work.

Gosling's bottom line is this:

**❝ THE REAL POWER OF JAVA TECHNOLOGY IS 'CONNECTING.' AND WHEN YOU GET PEOPLE CONNECTED, GOOD THINGS HAPPEN. ❞**

No matter what happens to the Java platform, with the help of the community it is here to stay, constantly expanding and saying "Hello" to all-new worlds, wherever technology may go.

# AFTERWORD

# Credit Due All, A Team that Became a Community

Throughout the interviews that created this book, each member of the Java team has emphasized that while a handful of team members are highly visible and in the public eye, Java technology is the result of thousands of dedicated, hard-working members. Most of the people interviewed were hesitant to talk at first because they were reluctant to take any credit for individual efforts.

In a sentiment echoed over and over again, what started with a small team was an all-out, all-team effort. What grew into a Sun division was a unified workforce. What became a community was an all-volunteer collective of individuals from a wide variety of large and small companies and universities. And finally, what has now become "the Java Universe," after ten years, is the work and enthusiasm of thousands of educators, authors, administrators, and business people, nearly five million developers, and hundreds of millions of users.

HERE ARE JUST SOME OF THE MILLIONS OF PEOPLE WHO HAVE CONTRIBUTED TO JAVA TECHNOLOGY OVER THE LAST 10 YEARS...

Casey Cameron **Matt Volpi** Jiangli Zhou **Mary Vincent** Elizabeth Kontur **John Muhlner** Albert Leung **Johnny Chen** Kevin L. Wong **Hideya Kawahara** Nigel Jacobs **Su Myong** Jean Elliott **Prashant Dighe** David Cox **Murali Nandigama** Ryan E. Kennedy **Michael W. Romanchuk** Brad R. Wetmore **Hinkmond Wong** Kenneth Lui **Madhava Avvari** Christopher B. Webster **Sathish Bhat** Gemma Watson **Xiaobin Lu** Prakash Narayan **Bernd Mathiske** Pete Levins **Ethel Emmons** Jeri Lockhart **Daniel Graves** Julie Osier **Alejandro Medrano** Kyle Buza **Craig R. McClanahan** Joe Nuxoll **Martin Buchholz** Tammy Chan **Serge Burlyga** Alexey Shurygin Pawel Veselov **Shivakumar Govindarajapuram** Rajiv Mordani **Ludovic Champenois** Scott Seligman **Jonathan Gibbons** Jerome Dochez **Michael Bender** Beomsuk Kim **Venkatesh Narayanan** Shakeel Rehman **Annette Wagner** Harold Ogle **Rich Sharples** Jerry Driscoll **Bartley Calder** Konstantin Boudnik **Yuka Kamiya** Shreedhar Ganapathy **Julie Matsumoto** John Coomes **Craig Russell** Eduardo Pelegri-Llopart **Sathyan Catari** Craig Conover **Jie Lin Leng** Raj Premkumar **Naoto Sato** Dan Baigent **Brian Kurotsuchi** Sandeep Konchady **Gregg Sporar** Ed Julson **Phillip "Flip" Russell** Jennifer Belissent **Adam Cohn** Frank Curran **Xueming Shen** Aseem Sharma **Rahul Biswas** Gopal Kumarappan **Nicholas Sterling** Susan Roach **Patrick Hubbard** Brent Loschen **Karen Shipe** Gowri Sivaprasad **Pierre Delisle** Harsha Rai Godugu **Aditya Dada** Ed Washington **Peter B. Kessler** Nicholas Kassem **Winston Prakash** Ken Poje **Farrukh Najmi** Harpreet Singh **Vipul Gupta** Senthil Chidambaram **Tom Childers** Kohsuke Kawaguchi **Brent Christian** Tony Ng **Ramesh Mandava** Sreeram Duvur **Tim Cramer** Terena Chinn-Fujii **Janet Koenig** James Melvin **Homer Yau** Tanjore Ravishankar **Tim Boudreau** Greg Simons **David Katleman** Bruce Hartford **Stanley M. Ho** Y. Srinivas Ramakrishna **Srikanth Ramakrishna**

Dave Dice **Mandy Chung** Tim P. McCollum **Dmitri Trembovetski** Florian Tournier **Manpreet Singh** Vivek Pandey **Gary Cole** Robert Brewin **Melanie Meyer Sommer** Pamela Sherwood **Sean Koontz**

Dean Long **Mark Herring** Jami Ediger **Michelle Kovac** Bill Sheppard **Francis Hsu** Nicolas Lorain **Kaithern Hyndschaw** Pratik Parekh **Carlos J. Herrera** Sanjay Dhamankar **Martin Lister** Glenn Skinner

**Sharat Chander** Roger Pease **Michael Munn** Hans Hrasna Jagadesh **Babu Munta** Jeannette Hung **W. Brian Leonard** Bill Pittore **Igor Kushnirskiy** Binu John **Chet Haase** Rajesh Sao **Jerry Evans**

Glen Chen **Chris Atwood** Rochelle Raccah **Geetha Nazare** Charles Beckham **David Hofert** Karen Arnett Land **Tao Lu** Neal Civjan **Chris Campbell** Li Gong **Daniel D. Daugherty** Naresh Persaud

**Richard Li** Roger Nolan **John (jbob) Bobowicz** Jacques Belissent **Kathy Walrath** Xiaojun Zhang Shing **Wai Chan** John Morrison **Praveen Mohan** Jonathan Benoit **Sreejith A K Narendra** Lahoti

Sandhya More **Charathram Ranganathan** Shobana Mahadevan **Jitender Singh** Nelson Dcosta **William J. Harnois** Xin Wu **Steve Fleming** Govind Ramasamy **Sundaranathan Sivashanmuganathan**

Manish Kr Gupta **Shigemitsu Ohtani** Ken Drachnik **Damon LaCaille** Irfan Ahmed **Arun Gupta** Michael C. Albers **Anand Murugesan** Ranbir Mazumdar **Kunal Sinha** Johnson Fernandes **Andrey**

**Pikalev** Sameer Tyagi **Srinivas Mandalika** Laurie Tolson **Ashwin Mathew** Vadim Morgunov **Rahul Shah** Victor Rudometov **Gaurav Kumar** Oleg Sukhodolsky **Shahar Muky** Alexandre Berman

**Nour-Eddine Djadel Anupam** R. Olivier Oudghiri **Alexander Fedunov** Martin Matula **Roger Lewis** Konstantin Romanovskiy **Kevin P. Smith** Binod PG **Vladimir Yaroslavskiy** Luis-Miguel Alventosa

**Amit Harel** Alexander Glasman **Darren Kenny** Victor D'yakov **Yo Ohara** Øyvind Bakksjø **Nachi Periakaruppan** Ian Formanek **Poonam Bajaj** Alexey Popov **Ohad Hageby** Jeremy Hoyland

Adam Sotona Vikas Desai **Ludovic Poitou** Alexander Potochkin **Shlomo Swidler** Vincent Ryan **Milan Kubec** Fedor Romanov **Jiří Skřivánek** Ian Sharratt **Helen Cullum** Zahid Syed

**Karel Zikmund** Robert Demmer **Thomas Pfohe** Sergey Grinev **Bart Jonkers** Vladimir Voskresensky **Evgeny A. Polovnikov** Kirill Kounik **Simon Vienot** Sergey Masharsky **Balchandra Vaidya**

Etienne Remillon **Martin Grebac** Jesse Glick **Ananthram A.S Kanishk** Jethi Jitender **Singh Pardeep Sharma** Andrei Dmitriev **Ramkumar SG** Sandra Belshaw **Andrey Ivanov** Dmitri Chiriaev

**Vitaly Sigov** Alexander Kouznetsov **Hua Zhang** Naveen Asrani **Jan Becicka** Douglas Donahue **Stephan Bergmann** Dimas Oliveira **Keith McGuigan** Robert Eckstein **Gary Collins** Vasily Isaenko

**Amit Handa** Petr "Nenik" Nejedl **Shreyas Kaushik** Kanwar Oberoi **Olga Tykuchinskaya** David Delabassee **Terrence Barr** Alex Yatsenko **Jim Connors** Andy Herrick **Maneesh Sharma** Pete Soper

**Scott Stillabower** Andrew Beairsto **Steve Caruso** Joe Fialli **Ashesh Badani** Stephen Fitch **Kenneth Saks** Simon Ritter **Vivek Nagar** Gautham Muthuravichandran **Peter Strarup Jensen** David Van

Couvering **Calum Benson** Lance Andersen **Veronique Alaton** Vikram Kunchala **Prakash Aradhya** Swamy Venkataramanapp **Kim Wilson Buck** Graham Hamilton **Dan Greff** Sridhar Reddy

**Arseniy Kuznetsov** Robert Vandette **Brian Beck** Aaron Williams **Nicholas Crown** Patrick G Curran **Ed Mooney** Lark Fitzgerald **Ken Frank** Andy Gilbert **Dan Roberts** Geoff Halliwell **Navaneeth**

**Krishnan** Michael McMahon **Ann Sunhachawee** Ashwin Ramanathan Joachim **Andres Santiago Pericas-Geertsen** Curt Carter **Jonathan M. Lee** Barton George **Mick Jordan** Eileen Bugée Sandip

**Vasant Chitale** Antonio Plutino **Rajiv Chamraj** Mary Artibee **Po-Ting Wu Ana Lindstrom-Tamer** Hong Lin **E-ming Saung** Jeet Kaul **Viktor Lapitski** Brian Samms **Dale Yoakum**

Tim Lindholm **Sangeeta Powaku** Jeff Nisewanger **Saul Wold** Eric Bergman **Larry Hoffman** PCM Reddy Sheryl Brandt **Tori Wieldt** James Gosling **Leif Samuelsson**

Dianna Yee-Stauffer **Chris Nadan** Peter Cattaneo **Mark Reinhold** Micheline Nijmeh **Pat Cashman** Alan Chu **Atul Batra** Rob Patten **Azeem Jiva** Cathy Horton **Gail Chappell** Francine Jackson-Price

**Debi Rose** Mechelle Torre **Norbert Lindenberg** Jerry M. Ashford **Yoojin Hong** John Wetherill **Bing Xia** Masayoshi Okutsu **Dmitri Trounine** Alexey Akopyan **Bonny M. Warjri** Lukas Hasik **Jack Catchpoole** Eamonn McManus **Irina Kuchkova** Andrey Komarov **Mukesh Garg** Stephen DiMilla **Alexander Zuev** Emily Suter **Timothy Quinn** Alvina O'Neal **Hamidul Haque** Graham Hares **Amy Fowler**

Chuck Rasbold **Sean Mullan** Jason Horowitz **Ron Goldman** Denis Mikhalkin **Heather VanCura** James Bisso **Aditya Gore** Vikas Awasthi **Smitha Prabhu** Nishant Patel **Alexander Doroshko** Sergio Blancato **Amit Bakhru** Richard Miedzinski **Mick Fleming** Kyle Grucci **Lauren Zuravleff** Andrea Scuffos **Betsy Hansen** Bill Shannon **Ankur Saha** Steven Liu **Susan Peterson** Devananda Jayaraman

**David Herron Josh Bloch** Richard Tuck **Konstantin Zolotnikov** Jim Holmlund **Marguerite Michels** Tamir Shabat **Mark Hapner** Pradeep Gond **Shai Almog** Srikar Sagi **Alexey A. Kornev** Sigal Duek

**Mayuresh Nirhali** Lukas Jungmann **Ryan Shoemaker** Robert Bissett **Stephan Schäfer** Patrick Tibbetts **Manveen Kaur** Marty Itzkowitz **Abhijit Das** Petr Hrebejk **Inderjeet Singh** Carla Schroer

**Mani Chandrasekaran** Chris Drake **Praveen Savur** Alexey Ushakov **Shannon Hickey** Christopher J. Kriese **Wendy Yamaguma** Dmitriy Ivanov **Brian Doherty** Ngoc Dung **Michelle Nguyen**

Joshua Marinacci **Kalpana Karunamurthi** Cori Kaylor **Darryl Mocek** Dean Polla **Sreeram Duvur** Raghavan 'Rags' N. Srinivas **Maya Berman** Vasif Pasha **Jean-Marie Boulard** Ian F. Darwin

Dean QuaRoeRmaine Jeffrey R. Haskovec **Drew Bradley** Declan McAleese **Mark McKenzie** Stephen Bartels **Kevin Himka** Alan Deehr **Randy Hanford** Marcelo Todd **Ciro de la Fuente Cabanelas**

Alvaro Maso **Venugopal Iyengar** Rakesh Aggarwal **Ryan Charles Chase** Mikael Boman **Akos Jancsik** Tamas Zsemlye **Gyula Agardi** Darla van Nieukerk **Scott Fischbein** Louis Fu **Bau Chong**

Keith N. Waltz III **Michael J. Eddy** William S. Gaes **Joeri Leemans** Stijn Van den Enden **Elke Steegmans** Kenneth Peeples **Amit P. Amte** Harold J. Shinsato **Carlos Cesar Dutra** Jo-Lan Chen

**Andrew Elegante** Charlotta Grunditz **Adam Skogman** Steve Elliott **Sanam Mehta** Brent Newman **Jeffrey D. Crownover** David L. Brouse **Tantastik Quach** Martin Desrosiers **Barry Fox** E. Andrew

Johnson **Howard Dyckoff** Mark Francis Villa **Sassan Soheili** Daniel Carlberg **Mike Kopack** David Resseguie **Thomas E. Sims** Keith holdaway **Mark Little** Kevin Conner **Danese Cooper** Gilmar Souza

Jr. **Bruno Ferreira de Souza** Juggy J. Finch **Patrick Chung** Justin TF Yao **Piniti Herve** Bodjona Krsto Sitar **Anne Fyk** Sal Campana **Ian P. Springer** Jason Lenhart **Graeme Tozer** Thad P Holly **Michael**

**L. Giroux** Trent Shue **Momodou Sanyang** Clark Anthony **John Zittlau** Luiz Felipe **Sa Leitao** Guimaraes Roberio **Gomes Patricio** Euclides N. Arcoverde Neto **Thomas Edwin Long** Kristofer R. Davison

**George E. Fisher** Anthony Rumsey **Anand Pandey** Isaac de la Peña Ambite **Russ Jubenville** John Thayer **Sultan Hekmatullah** Ghaznawi Victor Ortega **Haavard Kverneland** Colin Wilson-Salt **Sandeep**

**Bhagavatula** Lamar F. Channell **Dean Tanabe** Chockiah suresh **Marion Graham** Melissa Neimeyer **Stu Belden** John A Kline **Philippe Andre** Jens Henrik **Gabe Claus** Arnum Jensen **Jack A. Gidding**

Tom Hansen **Theodore Casser** Greg Reckenwald **Rob Ross** Rob Weaver **Martin Tiinus** Kristian Erendi **Andreas Folkesson** Blake McCarty Macon **Andrew Wadycki** Mike Swaby **Brian Mason**

Garry S. Bernal **Yuan Fan** Vinh Vu **Ivar Grimstad** Jacob D. Parr **Aleksey Shcherbakov** Marek Salwa **Konstantin Novoselov** Ryan Kanno **Satish Chenchalavahi** Seán Goggin **Harish Chakravarthy**

Ulf Brehmer **Aki Ruohonen** Hannu Honkala **Andy Tripp** Qusay Mahmoud **Tri H. Nguyen** Urayoan Irizarry **Thanachart Numnonda** Dean Quartermaine **Bryan E. Sampieri** Steven Swimmer **Kevin Kane**

Emily Suter **Janne Sormunen** Rudy Jahchan **Ron Albeck** Peter Nordén **Andrea Sandberg** Christo Tonev **Alan Zeichick** Justin Ray **Akehurst Robert** McInroy Sharat **Chander Henning Tolpinrud**

Arnt Schoning **Vikas Jain** Kevin Beams **David Patrone** Matthew O. Smith **Kent J. Christensen** Neda Sadeghi **Cedric Monnier** Jeffrey A. Risseeuw **Amol Desai** Octavian Tanase **Larry F. Wolpert**

Lisa M. Najarian **Eric B. Dalquist** J. Daniel Kingston Jr. **Tim T. Preston** Adrian Pang **Will Golesorkhi** Sai Chow **James Schofield** Sean Kellner **Abhishek Gupta** Laurence Mapp **Xian Peng Cheng**

Tom Rassmann **Jon Langlois** Mike Paleczny **Colin Madere** Sridhar Natarajan **E. Andrew Johnson** Esteban R. Briones **Sanjuan Panayot** Dobrikov Peter Kulka **Antonella Commiato** Timothy Ramey

**Ahmad Bushnaq** Peter Buchhop **Glenn Rodbarry** Eric Marcoux **Peter Allday** Lisa Meredith **Anne-Louise Finseth Nielsen** Niels Frydenholm **Gary Zellerbach** Adam J. Frazin **Steve Parinisi** Ronald

A. DeMena III **Andrew Siwko** Alka Gupta **Daniel deOliveira** Kim Schiller **Carsten Kring** David "Uncle Dave" Moffat **Albert B. Poor** Bill Bennett **Eirik Torske** Hideyuki Otokawa **Norm Martin** Tom

Goguen **Christopher Ratcliffe** Megan Meyer **Zsolt Fabos** Karoloy Szittner **Andreas Ebbert** Keith Brown **M. R. Pamidi** Maryanne Berezny Smith **Susan Zhang** Jim Farley **Jim Turk** Kurt Lenfesty

**Madurai Rajagopalan** Bruno Antunes **Lien Duong** Fred de Gier **Amy Savidge** Gabriel Floyd **Vincent Lam** Marc Hadley **Kevin Yager** John Phenix **Gregory Collis** Matthias Schorer **Grant Friel** Richard

Mateosian **Steve Dickson** Ben Rector **Robert J. McClean** Joseph B. Ottinger **Steven Palmaers** Nik Kishinoue **Sergio Del Rio** Tim Logan **Rohit Agarwal** Rajiv Rajaram **Shailesh Pai** Andrew Klein

**Eric J. Knapp** Bruce Sun **Sumit Chawla** Angie Tam **Santiago Zavala** Adam Nisenbaum **Douglas Harris** Mahen Partha **Kavindra Y** Toby Moreno **Phil Parkman** James A. Webb **Tony Kamarainen**

Ivan Posva **Gabriela Chiribau** Ronen Kahana **L. Umit Yalcinalp** Chad Carlson **Jeremiah Sulewski** Terry Kieffer **Akon Dey** Anil Madan **Ravi Veeramachaneni** Vicki Shipkowitz **Dhananjay Ragade**

Michael Seminaro **Christopher Mar** WJCarpenter **Gregory Dempsey** Robert M. Wolf **Brett Kemohah** Gary Woodbridge **Jake Gage** Oliver Charles Davies **Guy Kindermans** Shahid Alam **John Klouda**

Olivier Pepin **Bin Ni** Joel Gardet **Marko Salmela** Yihong Deng **Allen Mauricio Polo** Aaron Scifres **Felipe Leme** Leung Man Chi **Andre Toledo Piza de Moura** Lionel O. Rogers **Felipe Leme** Dorian

Hileaga **Darin Cummins** Eric Johnson **Chris Erickson** Patrick McKay **Gleidisdon Ferreira Duarte** Scott Cameron **Henry Ho** Jonas Flygare **D. Scott Horrocks** Jennifer L. Horrocks **James McKee**

Josh Canfield **David Dagastine** Bill Paris **Christoph Bernhofer** Johannes Schleicher **Peter Walker** Rupin Kotecha **Chandnka Kotecha** Rupesh Kotecha **Mona Kotecha** Steve Martinez **Alex Martinez**

Isabel Martinez **Athomas Goldberg** Adam Boyle **David B. Donahue** Louise To **Ray Y. Lam** Vanessa N. Wong **Ryota Yamada** Dennis Patrone **Adam J. Taub** Michael J. Carlin **Ramesh Nagappan**

Demetrios Kanellos **Scott Merical** Michael P. Milligan **Tom Oke** Par Siko **Conny Lundgren** Brian J Williams **Mike Potter** Rob Derstadt **Mandeep Sandhu** Michael McCullough **Tracy Bahm** Debbie Balles

**Lora Stephanchick** Gary W. Steffens **Matti Ryhanen** Joseph R. Wyrembelski **JP Petines** Jared White **Sachin Mahajan** Michael Haddox-Schatz **Jie Li** Russell Dittmar **Petr Panteleyev**

Virginia R. Hetrick (aka drjuice) **Anthony Scotney** Gina Assaf **Prashant Nedungadi** Ardaman Singh **Karthik Gajjala** SeaWolf **Gary Leask** Renee Steiner **Subramanian Kovilmadam**

Patrick Steranka **Rick Crow** Darrel Sell **Jens Peter Hedegård** Vijay Parikh **Michael Stopper** Hellmut Adolphs **Fabio Velloso** John (jbob) Bobowicz **Roger Fong** Diwakar Gupta **Kimmo**

**Loytana** Sharmila Pandith **Phil Parkman** P. H. Roberts **Laurel J. Sullivan** Bjorn Hjelt **Grant Mc Auley** Jon Byous **Sanjay Lobo** J. Darrel Thomas **Thomas W. Talbott Jr** Angel Dobbs-Sciortino **Richard**

**Williams** Jason Carter **Luba Kobzantsev** Leon Kobzatsev **Noushin Bashir** Mark Tallman **Clark D. Richey, Jr.** Nathan Carpenter **Anne Fyk** Krsto Sitar **Dorian Hileaga** Mats Wessberg **Gunnar Lofgren** Anissa

**Lam Jeffrey D Crownover** Sunny Gleason **Rob Glasener** Xin Chen **Barry Burd** Steven H. Lin **Markus Haseneder** Daniel Gredler **Sri Varadarajan** Edwin Park **Eric Lewis** Scott C. Schank **Dan J. Benton**

Christian Robitaille **Chico Charlesworth** Phil Holland **Thomas "the Yeti" Gould** Frederic Gidouin **Bruce Bergeson** Mike Swaby **Arjan Schaaf** Kumar Chebrolu **Nestor D. Rodriguez** Mattias Karlsson

**Marc Cannava** Dharmesh Chhagan **Paloma Sol** German Padilla **Steve Orin** Mario Cormier **Javier Galindo** John Jairo Lopez **Venkata Narasimha** Rao Kunduru **Massimo "Max" Lanfranconi** Akash

Pandya **Xue Chen** Garpur Dagsson **Jarad Duersch** Jay Ashworth **Takeshi Sato** Benno Christen **Stefan Riesen** Raymond A. Cardillo IV **Joel Neely** Alexander P. Mustard Jr **Jimmy J. Chung**

Sanjeev Agrawal **Srikanth Koka** Gregory L. Anderson **Daniel Lee Brookshier** Rehman Adil **Justin Rhodehouse** Jin Yoon **Ole-Martin** Mørk Pankaj Patel **Jon A. Batcheller** Jean F. Tordella **Geoffrey**

**A. Morton** Telly Stroumbis **Madhusudana R. Papireddy** Krista Kasten **Doug Meil** Richard Yee **Prasad Vadivelu** Chai YongChun **Andrea O. K. Wright** Chuck Buhecker **Leigh Jin**

Peter Snellman **Cris J. Holdorph** Bart Fuller **Jaya Elumalai** Rana Bhattacharya **Srikanth Gandra** Mark Conda **Joel Merrin** Omar Halaseh **Muhannad Obeidat** Sona Dube **Roel Simons**

Kim Topley **Natalie Rassmann** Daniel Stollenwerk **Albert Y. Leung** Kentaro Takahashi—BR **David A. Rogers, II** Patricia Moffat **Steve N. Anderson** Kasia Trapszo **Robert Ritler** Seetharama Avadhanam

**Carlos Alberto Mateus** Raul Duenas **Tonx Santizi** Tal Givoly **Richard Dallaway** Gareth Floodgate **Paul Goulbourn** Jono **Jean-Philippe Courson** R Scott Brown **Kapil Khanna** Phillip Ward

**Antonio Santos** Steve Dussinger **Jackie Hale** Bruce Robb **Corneil du Plessis** Timothy Casper **Burkhardt T. Hufnagel** Srinivasan Sairamachandran **Calvin Cheung** Brian C. Edwards **Kevin S. Jackson**

Jim Wheeler **Andy H. C. Wong** Aurelien Cuzzolin **Aubra C. Funk II** Marina Luwel **Douglas Phair** Belinda Garcia **Robert Varttinen** Magnus Kastberg **Jorge Kazuo** Diego Andrade Catta Preta

**Arnaud Cormier** Darlene Hopkins **Paulo Lujan Montelongo** Sreeram Duvur **Neven Cvetkovic** Adib Saikali Tamas Doszkocs **Nicholas Eichmann** B. Scott Andersen **Sonny S. Kim** Eric Lewis **Edwin**

**Park** Epelman Felix **Barry Kleinman** Ramana Lavu **John Yeary** Rob Nielsen **Rubina Jiwani** Todd Adams **Rama Seshadri** Ted Dancescu **Alfonso Davila de Icaza** Scott Ciabattari **Sarah Kornfeld**

Joe McMahon **Josh Kitterman** Jon Harley **Garry F Rasko** Justin Laby **Roland Davis** Einar Saukas **John E. Townsend** Melissa Marier **Gregory J. Woodfill** Antonia Ondo-Estokova **Jon C. Ericson** Amir

Housseini **James Velasco** Tom K Ranheim **Daniel López** Janáriz Fabiane **Bizinella Nardon** Douglas Patrone **Erik Bergersjo** David Sechrest **Jon Caulfield** Francisco Castrillo **Andy T. Huey** Niels Ull

Harremoës **Andre Fonseca** Ben Houston **Justin Zealand** Paul Koerber **Greg Bollella** Jonathan G. Damron **Ernie Svehla** Gary Freeman **Kalpana Subbarao** Simo Arajarvi **Andrzej Buszko**

Tonie Santos **Xinqiang Qi** David Most **Jason DeGeorge** Antti Karanta **Sankar Ram Sundaresan** Keoki Wai Hoong Young **Alex Kalinin** Ronald W. Lee **Tanner Ratzlaff** Joel Marlow **Matt Palensky**

Mike Waughn **Harish Krishnamurthy** Matt. Miller **Thomas Logue** Jean-Luc van Hulst **Brian Charles Beck** Kevin Sit **Alvar Lumberg** Janno Siilbek **Ian Littlewood** Aaron Conner **John Daniel**

Rich Cohen **Anjali Anagol-Subbarao** Cliff Archibald **Rama Pulavarthi** Brian Knotts **Tim O'Konski** Joshua Wilder **Gabriel Pereira** Jose Manuel Estrada **Patricia de las Heras** Jacqueline Thomas

**Mark Edgington** Robert J. Hall **Muguet Bradbury** Daniel Green **Dave Repshas** Michael Van Riper **Martin Welsh** Dmitry Torba **Ken Oestreich** Shashidhar Pullakandam **Doug Serres** Syed Moid

**Robert Harr** Kyle Forster **Priya Vasudevan** Mani Sivagnanam **John Ranta** Ji Eun Kang **Denis Robert** Deepesh Khandelwal **Manoj Joshi** Jason Mathews **Phuong T. Nguyen** Rogerio Meneguelli

**Gatto Thor** Henning Hetland **Hong Ji** Tathiana Coria **Radhika Nadimpally** Alex Hoeksma **Senthilnathan Arunagirinathan** Geetha Shanmugasundaram **Allan Van Schaick**

**Doug Bateman** Kito D. Mann **Srinivasan Sairamachandran** Sudha P. Vuyyuru **Jim Duffy** Greg Shipmon **Moumita Nandi** Srinivas Gundeaboina **Janani Thanigachalam** Petri Reiman **Benjamin C.**

**Leadholm** David C. Rose **Deborah L. Plochocki** Michael Shun King Yuan **Jun Wang** Steven F. Harris **Kenrick Chien** Kumar Chebrolu **Vaishnavi Mannar** Magne Land **Stew Murrie**

Rupert Key **Mai Phan** J. Gregory Wright **Marko Väätänen** Aki Ojanperä **Elizabeth Kontur** Niklas Hjort **Fredrik Richter** Rhian Sugden **Eugene Belyaev** Ingrid Van Den Hoogen

**Thank You**.

The publisher offers excellent discounts on this book when ordered in quantity for bulk purchases or special sales, which may include electronic versions and/or custom covers and content particular to your business, training goals, marketing focus, and branding interests. For more information, please contact:

U. S. Corporate and Government Sales
(800) 382-3419
corpsales@pearsontechgroup.com
For sales outside the U. S., please contact:
International Sales
international@pearsoned.com

Visit us on the Web: www.phptr.com

Library of Congress Cataloging-in-Publication Data

Hello World(s)—From Code to Culture : A 10 Year Celebration of Java Technology / Sun Microsystems, Inc.
     p. cm.
     ISBN 0-13-188867-6
    1.  Java (Computer program language)—History.  I. Sun Microsystems.
     QA76.73.J38H456 2005
     005.13'3'09—dc22
                   2005021881

Text printed at R.R. Donnelley in Reynosa, Mexico
First printing, September 2005

**Key Contributors**
James Gosling
Graham Hamilton
Tim Lindholm

**Writers**
Jon Byous
Barton George

**Photographer**
Saul Lewis

**Creative Design**
Glenn Martinez
Sonderby Design

**Project Managers**
Jami Ediger
Michelle Kovac

**Contributors**
Alan E. Baratz
Casey Cameron
Randy Crihfield
Amy Fowler
John Gage
Martin Hardee
Mark Herring
Kevin Hughes
Jason Hunter
Bill Joy
Peter B. Kessler
Rhodes Klement
Onno Kluyt
Miko Matsumura
Scott McNealy
Ken Oestreich
George Paolini
Simon Phipps
Myrna Rivera
Eric Schmidt
Carla Schroer
Mary Smaragdis
Guy Steele
Courtenay Troxel
Heather VanCura
Ingrid Van Den Hoogen
Laura Ventura
Wendy Yamaguma